The Art of Midlife Stress Busting

*Seven Steps to Declutter Your Mind
Without Pills or Potions*

Kay Newton

Copyright © Kay Newton 2017

All Rights Reserved

No part of this book may be reproduced in any form, by photocopying or by any electronic or mechanical means, including information storage or retrieval systems, without permission in writing from both the copyright owner and the publisher of this book.

The author has done her best to present accurate and up-to-date information in this book, but cannot guarantee the information is correct or will suit your particular situation.

Limit of Liability and Disclaimer of Warranty: The publisher has used its best efforts in preparing this book, and the information provided herein is provided "as is".

Medical Liability Disclaimer: this book is sold with the understanding that the publisher and the authors are not engaged in rendering any legal, medical or any other professional services.

If expert assistance is required, the services of a competent professional should be sought.

Praise for *The Art of Midlife Stress Busting*

"Having felt a change was coming, I allowed fear to hold me back. Today you opened up my mind and helped me see things clearly. Thank you, Thank you, Thank you."
Sean Wadham, Colorado

"The things I have learned today will be integrated into my daily life and I now have a whole new way to look at life."
Linda Wright, Sussex

"I became aware of the things that were important to me - how to protect my space and give thanks each day for the adventure life gives me."
Joanne Maria, Mallorca

"This book is excellent for people who are looking at what they would like to change in their lives when they reach middle age. Or if they want to find their purpose in life. It's the sort of book that I would give my daughter, as it is simple, yet quite profound.

It is an excellent tool for starting the reader on the road to discovering themselves. Each chapter is like peeling an onion, and each layer reveals something more, until you reach the centre of the onion, which is your true self. The self that you have been neglecting until now, because you have been too busy to notice.

Many people reach what is known as a midlife crisis. This time can be painful, especially now in the 21st century when at the age of fifty, you could still have another lifetime ahead. It is a time when many people divorce, the kids leave home (if you're lucky!) and you wonder what you are going to do for the rest of your life. You may be asking "What now? What is life all about? Why am I here?

This book will give you the tools to find out in a very simple way. Patricia Cherry, UK

"I love this little book, it's a bit like a never-ending story, you get to the last
page and then you start all over again!
Great advice in easy-to-understand language on how to change the canvas
of your life, it does exactly what it says on the tin. I urge you to read it, this
lady knows what she's talking about."
Joy Shallcross, UK

"A great guide to how you can take back control of your life and really make the changes you want to make. Easy to follow and in practical steps so you can see your progress. Get painting today!"
Hilary Stringer, UK

"I loved this book and completed my Stress-Busting week and saw immediate changes in my life. The FREE gifts included were a huge help too. Worth every penny and more."
Louise Busfield, UK

"This book offers a method of analysing where you are in your life, and deciding on whether or not it is where you want to be. Feeling 'stuck' in your present life situation is stressful, and after focusing and perhaps simplifying you

can reduce that stress by making necessary changes towards being more satisfied with your life. I agree that this is a task that is never completed, but needs to be constantly re-evaluated and changed as required .... an ongoing work-in-progress.

I think this process is well documented, and someone who is feeling 'stuck' would greatly benefit by following it."
Kathy McGaffrey, USA

Acknowledgements

Thanks to Ian and Vanessa of Greenwave Promotions, who have been on an editing journey with me for the past two years. I am grateful for their continued guidance, nudging me further down the road to greatness.

A big thank you to Marie Tillbert for the awesome book cover design.

To all my peeps, who keep me motivated and get me out of bed in the morning with words of encouragement and inspirational stories.

And finally to the four men in my life. I love them very much: James, Max, Tom and Steven.

About

Kay is an award-winning international speaker, enthusiastic author, blogger, artist and Midlife Stress Buster, whose clients love her straight talking and practical stress-relieving holistic help and support.
Kay's books include:

How to Clean Your Home Organically - De-Stress Your Surroundings

Tips And Tricks For Stress-Free Downsizing - A Step by Step Guide to Moving On

She co-authored the ebooks in the *Quick Fix For* series, and is a contributing author to *Hot Women Rock* and *A Journey of Riches*.

Kay hails from Leeds in Yorkshire, England. In her early 20s, she jumped on board a 'gin palace' leaving Hull for sunnier shores in Spain, and refused to swim back. She set up her own business looking after holiday homes for the rich and famous, became an eco-landlady extraordinaire, and the mother of two boys. She has been married for over 25 years.

In 2015, after a 30-year dream life on the Spanish island of Mallorca, Kay and her husband decided that rather than having an empty nest, they preferred 'no nest'. Leaving their two grown boys to fend for themselves, they decluttered and downsized to a two-roomed house with a tin roof next to a pristine beach on the island of Zanzibar, off the coast of Tanzania. Kay now lives a life free of unnecessary stress, and has never been happier.

Beachcombing one day, she decided it's time to focus on ridding the Boomer generation of unnecessary stress. She founded the Midlife Virtual Retreat, a weekly online session to relax, rejuvenate and have fun. You can join her here
https://www.facebook.com/TheMidlifeStressBuster/

You can also find Kay Newton The Midlife Stress Buster here
https://www.kay-newton.com/

Content

[Foreword](#) 12

[Introduction](#) 14

Definition of a Stress Busting Artist
What You Have To Do

[Step One - Become Aware](#) 17

Tasks For Today
Step One Recap – Become Aware

[Step Two - Having The Right Tools](#) 23

Doing the Work and Buying the Right Paint
Tasks For Today
Step Two Recap - Having The Right Tools

[Step Three - Avoiding The Two Ps, Perfectionism and Procrastination](#) 29

Ready, Fire, Aim!
The Two Ps: Perfectionism and Procrastination
Tasks For Today
Step Three Recap – Avoiding The Two Ps

[Step Four - Avoiding Sufficient Syndrome](#) 35

Finished!
Tasks For Today
Step Four Recap – Sufficient Syndrome

[Step Five - Redecorating and Starting Anew](#) 40

Tasks For Today
Step Five Recap – Redecorating and Starting Anew

[Step Six - Becoming A Grand Master](#) 47

Becoming A Grand Master
Tasks For Today
Step Six Recap – Becoming A Grand Master

[Step Seven - Preparing For The Future](#) 52

Full Circle
Tasks For Today
Step Seven Recap – Preparing For The Future
Conclusion

Resources 59

Recommended Reading
Other Books by Kay

Foreword

Stress is considered a leading cause of death in people over 50. Midlifers have a lot to deal with: ageing parents, empty nests, boomerang kids, worries over pension shortfalls, mortgages or health care plans, caregiving, the loss of a loved one, ill health, divorce, moving home, loneliness, isolation - the list seems endless.

In the US alone, 1 in 10 people over the age of 45 are thought to suffer from stress-related anxiety and depression. Worries about money, work, politics, the economy, relationships, health, and personal and national security are cited as causes. (https://www.apa.org/news/press/releases/stress/2011/final-2011.pdf)

Many at midlife feel stressed, trapped in a downward spiral they can't escape. It's said that women suffer from stress more than men. The constant need to consume and hoard, and a tendency to live amongst clutter also contributes to stress. A sedentary lifestyle and unhealthy eating habits add their two-penn'orth to a general feeling of dissatisfaction with our lives.

The medical profession treats stress and anxiety by prescribing anti-depressants, which in turn cause other health issues. The good news is that with a little work midlifers can glide gracefully into old age, feeling calmer and more content, whilst embracing the concept of being Sensibly Selfish.

Sensibly Selfish is all about giving yourself permission to be the first priority, for the highest good. When you put yourself first, you can focus on your own well-being, and thus be in the right place energetically to be able to help others. Just like in the aircraft emergency protocol, you have to put on your own oxygen mask before you can help others.

Introduction

Welcome to *The Art of Midlife Stress Busting*.

Do you know that you are the most amazing artist? We usually think of famous art masters as people such as Picasso, Monet, Renoir and Michelangelo, yet each day you add more paint to *your* very own canvas, your Life Canvas.

We often forget that we have the wonderful ability to create exactly what we want in our lives. It's so easy to become stuck in hectic, stressful daily routines and forget about our canvas. When we neglect our own canvas, we can easily fall into negative thoughts and feelings. Then we're on a downward spiral of stress and anxiety.

Putting our own life on hold to spend time making other people happy is like putting the cart before the horse. Remember the aircraft emergency protocol, "If you don't put the oxygen mask on yourself first, you're not going to be able to help anyone else!"

It's so easy to forget that we are the centre of our own universe. If there's something wrong with our canvas, we must do something about it. No one else will do the work for us. Now is the time to take small steps in the right direction.

This book will help you to *Declutter Your Mind* and become a *Stress Busting Artist In Just Seven Steps*. We will look at:

- Awareness
- Having the right tools
- Learning to Ready, Fire, Aim

- Avoiding the two Ps, *Perfectionism* and *Procrastination*
- Avoiding *Sufficient Syndrome*
- Redecorating and starting anew
- Becoming a Grand Master
- Preparing for the future

Definition of a Stress Busting Artist

Being *Sensibly Selfish* means getting exactly what you need, so you are then able to serve others in the best way. Sounds easy, right? However, it requires a great deal of perseverance. To declutter our mind so we can paint the life we want, we have to act in accordance with our desires and passions. Authentic_desires are a form of energy connected to our divine self; they never result in actions that harm us.

To be a Stress Busting Artist, we must paint our canvas in a *Sensibly Selfish* manner, with unconditional love and acceptance. Painting with the right tools will create abundance in our life and in our relationships. When we stop actively painting our canvas with the things that bring us joy, then anger and resentment fill the void. We pass this negativity on to those around us, especially to those we love the most.

A Stress Busting Artist knows that stress is part of life. It can't be avoided. Trying to avoid stress is impossible and self-destructive. Instead, stress should be harnessed and embraced. By decluttering your mind and painting your mind's canvas to the best of your ability you will be able to deal with stressful events as they occur, take steps to make changes, increase your resilience, ask for help and deepen relationships with others.

What You Have To Do

Take the steps day by day. It's better to go slowly, rather than trying to do everything at once. Give yourself time to take the new information on board, so you can make changes to your life that will last forever.

In order to create your Life Canvas, I recommend reading a section each day. Then allow yourself time to do the exercises at the end of each chapter. Give yourself a good 20 minutes to sit quietly with pen, paper and your thoughts. Even better, download FREE *The Art of Stress Busting Companion* by clicking on the link below.

https://www.kay-newton.com/wp-content/uploads/Journal-Final.pdf.zip

When you have printed *The Art of Stress Busting Companion* you can use the spaces to jot down any immediate thoughts for use at a later stage.

You don't have to share your written work with anyone else. This is about you. If you have a 'Eureka Moment' and think it would help others, then by all means share it on the Kay Newton website or Facebook page if you wish. (You can find the links in the Resources section at the end of this book.)

Step One - Become Aware

"Creativity takes courage." Henri Matisse

In Step One we will look at awareness, the first stage for de-stressing, decluttering and making changes in your life.

Do you realise that living your life is the greatest artwork of all?

Did you know that the appearance of the Life Canvas you paint accurately reflects your true essence in the world?

We live such busy lives, we often don't take the time to stop and just *be*. We are human beings, not human doings! Ask yourself:

- What would it feel like if I just stopped and sat still for a while?
- Do I like to stop and do nothing, or do I find it uncomfortable?
- Do I sometimes get the feeling that I may have missed out on something?

Our minds take in so much information every second of our waking lives. We must filter out much of the information in order to function. It's important to declutter and clean our mind periodically, so we can function better. It's not surprising that if we don't stop to rest for at least part of each day, we will go into 'sensory overload', feel numb, and miss out on feelings and experiences.

Stop and sit down right now. Take a deep breath, and then another two. Now, look around, what do you see? Listen to the sounds around you. Touch something, feel its texture.

What smells are there in the room? Maybe take an object and taste it, perhaps for the first time. Be fully present with your senses.

- What did you notice about the feelings that this conjures up for you?
- Perhaps you became aware of something in a new way?

Make this awareness exercise a daily habit. It's the first step towards becoming a successful *Stress Busting Artist*.

You have been painting your life masterpiece since the day you were born. Your canvas has been influenced along the way by the journey of life itself. No one else has created a painting like yours. It's unique to you. You have filtered information, taken on values and beliefs, and had life experiences unique to you. It has become your fingerprint upon the world.

Here you are today. You are entirely responsible for the work of art you have produced. Take a step back and think about your canvas: if you are not happy with the scene in front of you, then change it. No one else can decide where to slap on a new coat of paint, where to redesign or begin anew, only you can do it.

Note: if you are leaving it to someone else to decide what paint goes where, then you are not even living. If you never thought about this, it's likely you won't have succeeded in changing anything in your life - yet.

Now is the time to have a really good look at that Life Canvas, in order to be *Sensibly Selfish*. You are important to YOU, first and foremost.

When you accept that you have put yourself where you are right now, for whatever reason, and that you are completely responsible, you can begin to change the bits you don't like. This is about you - but it also affects others. If you are not happy, then you will be passing on this unhappiness to those you love and care for most.

You are the only person in the whole world to see your original life's art work fully. It is inside the gallery of your mind. However, your external world/life is a mirror image of it, giving others clues to what you hold inside.

I repeat: whatever you paint within your mind will be reflected in the outside world. Are you happy with this image?

The effect you expect is the effect you get. For example, if you see everything as dark and gloomy within your mind's eye, you can guarantee that you and those around you will see the same dark colours in the outer world. You may have everything so dark you can't see what's in the corners of your painting. You may even be too stressed and scared to look.

Stress is part of who you are and is not to be feared. Rather, it needs to be harnessed and appreciated in order that you can become more confident when handling situations. Take time to become aware of your attitudes towards stress. Complaining, avoiding honest discussions, suffering in silence, or being negative will result in more stress.

Declutter, clean your mind and become a Stress Busting Artist. Take a good look at how you paint your life. Take a good deep look. This is not the time to be critical or pull yourself apart. It's time to simply accept who you are right now, at this moment.

Become aware of the things that work for you, the brush strokes that make you proud of yourself. If you are proud of certain things, you are bound to be disappointed by others. The universe is made this way. There are opposites for everything. There is nothing wrong with this.

We know that anyone can pick up a paintbrush and slap paint onto a canvas. In order for it to be regarded as a masterpiece, it takes many hours of practice. What you become aware of today is by no means a project for today alone. If you see a part of your canvas you would like to change then - like an artist - you need time to step back and consider what needs doing; what you might like to add, take away, or alter. These reviews and adjustments can become part of your daily routine for the rest of your life - until your masterpiece is finished.

Tasks For Today

Download and print out the FREE *The Art of Midlife Stress Busting Companion.*
Unless you wish to share the *The Art of Stress Busting Companion*'s contents, it is for your eyes only. Remember, if you are not first aware, how can you change anything? If you have never done this before you may feel uncomfortable. We often feel uncomfortable when we reach the edge of a comfort zone. This is a good sign. Keep going, and with a little perseverance, all will fit into place.
Be aware of resistance. This is also quite normal. If you have never controlled your mind's canvas, it means that someone else has. Your mind may put up a fight! Take note, but don't give in. If you want changes in your life, this is the way to paint a different picture.

Use the *The Art of Stress Busting Companion* to jot down your thoughts at random throughout the day. Become aware of what you think on a regular basis. We spend an awful lot of time repeating things inside our head. Listen calmly, and jot down what comes to mind. Do this throughout the day. Stop and listen to your thoughts to get a clear picture of how you tick. Without thinking about it, stop suddenly and take a peek inside. Do this at least six times today.

There are no right or wrong answers to this task. This is not the time to change anything, to blame, or make judgments or criticise. The key here is to be honest and write down what's occurring right now. There's no need to exaggerate or play down the thought. Write it as it is.

Note that from this day on you have begun a daily habit that will remain with you for the rest of your life: awareness. Nothing will change unless you make an effort to change it and nothing can change until you become aware of it.

You have worked hard today, and now it's time to give yourself a pat on the back and celebrate the day's journey in some way before you go to bed. Decide what you will do as a reward, and then make sure you do it.

Step One Recap – Become Aware

- Download and begin to use your FREE *The Art of Midlife Stress Busting Companion:*

https://www.kay-newton.com/wp-content/uploads/Journal-Final.pdf.zip

- Write down the feelings and thoughts raised by Step One
- Jot down your thoughts at random throughout the day, at least six times
- Become aware of what makes you tick, and where the sticking points may be
- Celebrate

Don't worry if you have found this task too difficult to do in just one day. And don't be afraid to ask for help. (See Resources.)

Today we have looked at defining awareness, and ways to declutter your mind so you can begin painting your Life Canvas differently. In Step Two, we will be looking at the tools you need in order to work on your Life Canvas.

Finally, I want to leave you with a question. What is the benefit of diving into the deep end of a swimming pool, and then remembering that you can't swim?
You will find my answer in Step Two!

Step Two - Having The Right Tools

"This world is but a canvas to our imagination." Henry David Thoreau

Yesterday we looked at becoming aware of ways to begin decluttering the mind, and how your Life Canvas works. Today we will focus on beginning the work to create a life masterpiece.

I find it fascinating that, as human beings, we often live day-to-day without truly noticing what's happening in our world. After reading Step One, the practice of becoming aware of what's going on inside your head has begun, and it will get easier. As you continue the work, you will see how powerful and life-changing it can be when you take note of your thoughts and everyday decisions.

Being aware is the greatest gift that you can give yourself.

If you have already read and implemented Step One, *Congratulations*.
If not, go back there now. DO NOT continue reading until you have completed the first tasks.

Yesterday I asked you the question:

'What are the benefits of jumping into the deep end of a swimming pool and then realising you can't swim?'

I'm sure you came up with many answers. The one thing I know, from personal experience about jumping into the deep end, is that you learn to swim fast!

How many dreams have you put on hold because you were waiting for the 'right moment' instead of just jumping in? Having a dream is just that, A DREAM. Changing a dream to a goal, a dream with a date, means you will focus daily on what you want to achieve.

In order to do this, you MUST write down what it is you want, in great detail, in an accurate, clear manner. As you read this, you might hear yourself say "I know that"... yet are you actually DOING IT?

Only 3% of the world's population write down their goals. They are the ones who have the happiest marriages, the most wealth and abundance in their lives. This does not mean they never suffer stress, just that they have found a way to create the responses they need so they can utilise stress to their advantage. Does this tell you something? Do you now want to have a mindset that uses stress for growth? Reading *The Art of Midlife Stress Busting - Seven Steps To Declutter Your Mind, Without Pills or Potions* will NOT CHANGE anything. Putting the principles into practice will. Today is about focusing on your goals. Find *The Art of Stress Busting Companion* and jot down your thoughts as you read.

Doing the Work and Buying the Right Paint

As children, we often remember painting a picture and proudly showing it to an adult. For some, this will be a pleasant memory and for others, it was a never-to-be-experienced-again sensation. Yet throughout our lives, we all paint.

We paint scenarios and pictures inside our heads which, regardless of whether we truly believe them or not, will become reality in our outside world. We can choose to paint our life as we want it to be, constantly learning new information and disregarding what doesn't serve us.

If we want to have a mind that is clutter-free, and paint a life masterpiece, we must first learn the fundamentals, establish the right foundations, and then use them to progress patiently from painter to master.

The problem is that most people only ever get to the first stage. Although they understand the principles, they would rather sit and discuss painting than actually get on and do it.

If you are not in the game, nothing will change.

Some will begin their artwork and get stuck in one corner, continuously changing minute details, while ignoring the rest of the canvas. Some will paint furiously and then step back, relax, admire and do nothing new, only to wonder at a later date why they haven't managed to change anything in their life recently.

The way you set about working on your Life's Canvas will determine how it looks. For example, letting the media decide your thoughts for you means your canvas will most likely be dark, negative and very stressful. Letting others decide for you will not make it any better. This is not a 'paint-by-numbers' class. You can't follow any other works of art past the first basic step.

This is about *you*, creating what *you* want, in the way *you* want to.
There is only one you.

You are the only one who can decide what colours to use, what to draw, what paintbrushes to use where, when and how, and what needs to be added or taken away. Only you will know if you can mix certain elements together. Yes, you may find that you make mistakes along the way. We all learn best from our mistakes. Mistakes mean that further down the path we will have the resources to deal with stress.

In order to be a *Stress Busting Artist* and create a masterpiece, you have to work progressively, on a daily basis. First of all, you have to decide what composition you want to paint. You need to have a goal in mind and see how you wish to create that goal. Then, perhaps you need to go out and learn something about that composition. You may need to ask for help and guidance.

First, you will want to create the foundations by doing a rough sketch, leaving space to decide what to include in the masterpiece and how to organise it. You may have to leave some sections until the right time; one day you will fill in those spaces.

You may have to alter sections, as and when the need arises, and you will need the confidence to do this without spoiling the balance of the painting. You will need to step back from time to time, so that you can view your masterpiece as a whole, with a new understanding, a new light or a new direction.

Work you must, every day, for the rest of your life. A daily brushstroke will keep your artwork in good condition. This is what Angela had to say:

"I had often thought I lived in a Karmic world. Everything that happened to me was beyond my control. My life was constantly stressful, yet when I began to read about

becoming my own midlife artist and began practising the art, extraordinary things began to happen.

"*As I sat patiently and began to think about something that I really wanted to achieve in my life, I became quite good at painting the scene in vibrant colours, in great detail. Within a few days, synchronicity meant that I would meet the person who would either help me with my goal, or would introduce me to someone who could fulfil the role.*

"*I became so confident at The Art of Midlife Stress Busting that I never doubted the right person would turn up. It just means that I need to have my eyes a little more open than I had in the past.*"

Tasks For Today

Look at the notes you made yesterday, and decide on one area of your thoughts that you wish to change.

Think of this as a part of your whole midlife masterpiece.

- How is it going to feel if you change this thought?
- What new enlightenment will it bring to you?
- What do you have to do to make it happen?
- Who do you need to ask for help?

Break down this task, answering the questions above, and then add a time limit. How long will it take to achieve? Don't be frightened here. Just hold in mind that you already know the answer. You just need to breathe a little deeper, be quiet and listen. Be realistic too; setting a short time span will create stress, and overestimating will waste time.

Which part of each day are you going to use to check your *Midlife Stress Busting* Artwork? I would recommend around 20 minutes a day. Commit to finding this time for the rest of your life. Jot this time down and make a commitment to yourself to spend this time each day getting nearer to your goals. At the beginning, to help get into the habit, make sure you put this time in your diary or mobile phone, or post it on the mirror or fridge.

Be aware of how much you have worked today. Give yourself a pat on the back and celebrate the day's journey in some way before you go to bed.

So how was that? Have you enjoyed the process so far, or are you struggling? Why not come and join us in The Midlife Stress Busting Facebook closed group where you're welcome to join in the discussion on the threads. (See Resources.)

Step Two Recap - Having The Right Tools

- Look at Step One's notes, and choose what to change
- Answer the questions above
- Put a time limit on the work
- Celebrate

Today we focused on the importance of laying the right foundation for your Life Canvas, and how to focus on the things you need to change. Tomorrow we will look at the importance of beginning the work, and what may stop you in your tracks.

Step Three - Avoiding The Two Ps, Perfectionism and Procrastination

"I dream my painting and then I paint my dream." Vincent Van Gogh

Yesterday we looked at the things you felt needed changing on your Life Canvas. Today we're going to look at making the changes, and what may stop you.

Now that you have read Day Two of *The Art Of Midlife Stress Busting – Seven Steps to Declutter Your Mind Without Pills or Potions* the biggest question is...

Have you begun to put the principles of the day into practice?

Remember it's not about reading, it's more important to DO the DOING!

- How *do* you change something in your life?
- How *do* you lose weight?
- How *do* you stop smoking?
- How *do* you change your career?
- How *do* you pay the mortgage?

Add whatever applies to you today to the above list.

So when you think of the changes you want to make in your life, do you find yourself thinking of all sorts of excuses? Are you distracting yourself from dealing with stressful situations? Do you know that avoiding the stress of doing something will actually reduce your well-being, life satisfaction and happiness? Listen in to what you are saying to yourself right now. Procrastination leaves many jobs undone and leads to dissatisfaction.

Perhaps it's not an excuse that holds you back, perhaps you find yourself going over and over the same thing in your mind, and not actually doing anything constructive that leads to change. If it hasn't worked so far, it's not likely to work. You need to find another solution.

You are, after all, only human (another excuse!). It can be hard to reach the edge of your comfort zone and make changes that push out the boundaries you have created. Many people prefer to stay where they are, even if it causes pain. They will only do something about it when the pain becomes unbearable.

You don't have to do this alone. Look around, and you can often see a shoulder to lean on, a guiding hand or a friendly face.

Get your notebook ready and jot down your thoughts as you read below.

Ready, Fire, Aim!

As a *Stress Busting Artist,* you have already looked at what's happening on your mind's canvas. You know what you need to change in order to paint differently. You have begun to put together a plan for the future, and today you will become aware of two blocks.

The Two Ps: Perfectionism and Procrastination

Perfectionism means doing something over and over again, trying to make it better each time. Extreme faultlessness is stressful, and debilitating. Do you remember painting something as a small child and thinking you needed to add just a little more colour, only to end up soaking the paper and making a hole and then throwing it in the bin?

Perfectionism stops you moving forward. There are never enough hours in the day if you continue to re-correct something for the sake of it. Nothing else on your Midlife Canvas will get a chance.

If the stress of perfectionism doesn't get you, then perhaps procrastination will.

Procrastination is the art of perfecting excuses for delays. Not getting on with things will definitely stall work on your masterpiece. Postponing for whatever reason, or leaving something for another day just adds more weight and pressure to those midlife millstones you are so proud to carry around your neck.

Please make a note of this in *The Art of Stress Busting Companion*.

Note to self: as human beings, we waste more time thinking about doing something than actually doing it.

How do most famous painters cover a blank white canvas? By picking up a brush and getting on with it, of course. We are always told that the name of the game is: ready, aim, fire. In reality what we need to do is: 'fire, aim, ready and then fire again'. This does not mean firing at random. It means firing towards your target, and making adjustments if you don't hit the bullseye the first time.

Get 'doing' something, anything1
Or as that famous sports brand implores... 'JUST DO IT!'

As a *Stress Busting Artist,* you are now aware of how your inner canvas affects your outer one. Take a look around you, and notice those who take great care with their inner painting and those who do not. Have the strength to realise that you have the potential, not only to change your own world, but also to change the world of those around you.

Remember: in order to change, you must be in the game.

We have such a short time on earth, and even if you believe in reincarnation, it won't be to this world here and now that you come back. There's no time to procrastinate or to be a perfectionist. It's time to act, react and react again.

Get out your dusters, brushes and paints and **Just Get Painting**. This is what Kerstin had to say:

"I was the best person I knew for perfectionism. Everything had to be just so. Perhaps I even erred on the side of having OCD (Obsessive Compulsive Disorder). It used to stress out everyone and drive them mental, including myself.

"My husband, on the other hand, was more of a procrastinator. His favourite words were always 'just now' which actually meant 'never'. Our issues were helping us go nowhere fast.

"I became a Stress Busting Artist *and my husband followed suit. We realised that as* Stress Busting Artists *we needed to work on our canvases daily. We feel this work actually saved our marriage."*

Tasks For Today

Be honest with yourself

- What do you procrastinate about?
- What do you repeat time and time again, attempting to make it better?
- What are you going to do about it?

Write your answers in the *The Art of Stress Busting Companion*. Look at your written statements and tell yourself, "If it's on my list, it has to be done". If this is true, what's stopping you from doing it?

If you have something on your list and have no intention of dealing with it, then it's time to cross it off the list, and leave yourself space to do something else. Take your pen and strike through the offending lines. How does this make you feel?

Look at the remaining list and decide what actions you are going to take right now. Write them down and make a plan of action.

Remember it's all about, 'ready, fire, aim' rather than 'ready, aim, fire'.

As a *Stress Busting Artist,* there is only one more thing to do:

Get on with it

Be aware of how much you have worked today. Give yourself a pat on the back and celebrate the day's journey in some way before you go to bed.

Step Three Recap – Avoiding The Two Ps

- Answer the questions about *Perfectionism* and *Procrastination*
- Define what you are going to do about it
- Celebrate

Today, we have looked at *Perfectionism* and *Procrastination* and how they can hold back your life's work. Tomorrow we will be looking at *Sufficient Syndrome*.

Step Four - Avoiding Sufficient Syndrome

"The aim of art is to represent not the outward appearance of things, but their inward significance." Aristotle

Yesterday we looked at *Perfectionism* and *Procrastination*, and today we will look at *Sufficient Syndrome*.

Sufficient Syndrome is when you decide that you've done enough work on your Life Canvas. It's time to sit back and relax. Sounds like this is the moment to de-stress, right? However, the problem is, you forget to go and revisit your life's canvas - until it's too late.

It's a bit like when we weed the garden and everything looks pretty again. So now all we have to do is sit back and admire the flowers, or perhaps forget about the garden entirely. Yet unless we visit that very same garden patch on a regular basis and pull up the tiny weeds as they appear, one day we will notice that the weeds are back, and there's an awful lot of work to be done. This is stressful.

Our Life Canvas is similar. We can't sit back and leave it to its own devices, or it will soon become dirty and discoloured. We have to keep working at it constantly. The more maintenance we do, even at midlife, the less time it actually takes to keep everything in tip-top shape. When you choose to work on your Life Canvas daily, your strengths become more apparent, you align with your values and grow, no matter what trauma comes your way.

Have *The Art of Stress Busting Companion* ready as you read below.

Finished!

Your canvas has a lot of paint on it, and your life is just how you want it to be. In fact, you are so happy with everything that you step back and sit on the grass to admire your canvas.

The only problem is that you admire and admire, and do nothing else. The more you relax, the harder it becomes to get up and do that niggling adjustment which needs to be done in the top left-hand corner, or dust off the cobweb which has begun to form.

Before you know it, your canvas is starting to look a little shabby, and things are not going the way you want them to. Stress and frustration set in. The more you ignore life, the more your canvas becomes dilapidated.

Now the problem is that it will take you a great deal more effort to get going on the artist's journey again. You have two choices at this crossroads: either you make that effort and put things right again, or you give up completely.

If you do make an effort, remember not to fall into the 'repair only' trap. Be careful, you will probably begin applying paint frantically to one piece of the canvas, only to find that repair is needed elsewhere. And when that is finished, even more paint has peeled in another area. You are so busy just repairing that nothing new is happening in your life. You are stuck. (We talked about *Perfectionism* yesterday. Make sure it's not your story.)

Yes, of course as a *Stress Busting Artist* you are allowed to sit and admire your life's work. Just don't sit on the grass for too long, or the next time you work on your Life Canvas you will need to spend a lot of time and energy before you begin to see results.

Be prepared, you may become disillusioned long before you see any results. Here's what Jenny had to say:

"I was so proud of what I had achieved by the age of 50. I had a successful career, three amazing grown kids, a wonderful husband and home. Then one morning I stopped painting my canvas. I sat and admired and admired and admired.

"I woke one morning at 54 and really looked at my Midlife Canvas. It seemed that only yesterday my canvas had been painted with beautiful colours. Now it was as if someone had sprayed black graffiti paint on it.

"For years I had sat on my laurels. Everything had declined right in front of my eyes, and I never really noticed. I had been deluding myself. I had a whole restoration job to do.

"Some of my canvas could not be salvaged; I had let it decline too far. My husband and I divorced, and I had to learn to paint alone for a while. Other pieces of my life's work of art needed so much care and love I thought I would never sleep again. It was all very stressful, yet I grew from the experience.

"I learnt my lesson the hard way. I know as a Stress Busting Artist *I can celebrate, take a rest, yet I never go a day without working on my canvas!"*

Tasks For Today

As a *Stress Busting Artist,* your task today is to define the areas in your life where you have become complacent.

- How will you know when you are not moving your life forward?
- What actions will you take to make sure you don't fall into the traps of *Sufficient Syndrome, Procrastination* or *Perfectionism*?
- What do you need to do to maintain your Life Canvas at its best?
- What do you need to change right now to make your life brighter?

Take a look at your beliefs and value systems. These change as we go through life, and in order to keep your canvas in top condition, you will need to revise them periodically. By knowing what your values are you can use them in stressful situations to put everything into perspective. Do you know your top ten values? (See the resource section at the end, for a link to the values exercise on the website). If necessary, you can seek help from a friend, or a professional. Who will you ask today?

Be aware of how much you have worked today. Give yourself a pat on the back and celebrate the day's journey in some way before you go to bed.

Step Four Recap – Sufficient Syndrome

- Answer the questions above
- Seek help to evaluate your beliefs and values, if necessary
- Celebrate

Today we have looked at the issues with *Sufficient Syndrome*. Tomorrow we will look at beginning your canvas again.

Step Five - Redecorating and Starting Anew

"Every child is an artist. The problem is how to remain an artist once we grow up." Pablo Picasso

Yesterday we looked at *Sufficient Syndrome*, and how it can hold back progress on your Life's Canvas. Today we will look at starting a new canvas from scratch.

It's important to paint your Life Canvas exactly the way you want it. It takes time and patience, so you can live your life to the full and help those you love to fulfil their roles too. Step back and look at the whole picture, so you can refocus on specific areas that need improving.

Stress Busting Artists know that there's nothing wrong with waking up one morning and deciding that they want to make a drastic change to their Life Canvas. A complete redecoration can be just what the doctor ordered. Redecoration is a form of decluttering. Maybe you even want to begin from scratch. If you are not happy with your Life Canvas for any reason, there's nothing to stop you throwing away your old painting, and beginning again.
There's nothing stopping you - except *you*.

There is nothing more exciting than the immediate thought of throwing in the towel and perhaps going to live on a desert island - until you put it into perspective. For example, would life on a desert island be such fun if you are the only person there, without water or shelter?

First, just take a minute. Take a long, deep breath. Take time to think and plan exactly what you want to achieve by changing your canvas.

Ask these questions:

- How will I do it?
- Who will help me?
- When and where will I begin?
- Who will it affect?

When you have started to look at the finer details of your plan, take a step away and look at it from all angles. Ask others to throw in their ideas (which of course you can take into consideration or not, it's entirely your choice).

- What have you missed out?

Then, as a *Stress Busting Artist* think ethically about your new grand design.

Ask yourself:
- Does it fit in with my values and beliefs?
- Will it affect my loved ones?
- Will it be in their best interests?
- How will it affect my community?
- How will it affect the planet as a whole?

When you are satisfied with all these answers you can go and buy your new paint and begin the process. Don't be surprised if it's a hard battle at first. Don't give in. Be strong in your conviction that it was the right decision. Don't hesitate, ask the universe to help you find what you need and you will create your new midlife masterpiece. Here is Anne's story...

"I had always wanted to retire abroad. It was something my husband and I talked about before we were married. When an opportunity came to move abroad to work, ten

years earlier than we had anticipated, we jumped at the chance.

"We sold up lock, stock and barrel, and moved within three weeks. It was the pits! Our friends and family had warned and pleaded with us, but we had taken no notice. We refused to be dissuaded by the fears of others. Life was so staggeringly different.

"Life wasn't the same, living permanently in our favourite holiday destination. For starters, we had to work! Living costs were expensive, and the local population not as friendly as they had seemed when we were lying on the beach with cocktails in our hands. We tried to make new friends, but just felt alienated. It was a nightmare. We had totally failed to plan and as they say 'failure to plan, is planning to fail'.

"I had destroyed my Life Canvas by burning it to come abroad. I had painted another to replace it, only to realise it was a fake. Now my canvas was totally wrecked, and my energies too low to paint another one.

"It took lots of help from people I trusted before I began to seriously apply new paint to my messed up Life Canvas. I could have saved a lot of upheavals if I had only listened to reason, my intuition and prepared my canvas correctly so that the new paint stuck."

Tasks For Today

Have you ever thought of just running away and beginning a new Life Canvas? Have you ever thought of changing every brushstroke and colour that you have used so far in creating your Life Canvas?

Just let your mind wander, and see where it leads you. Let this exercise last for as long as you can, take notes, and then review when you are sure there is nothing new coming up.

How does this make you feel?

- Are you excited or frightened?
- What has stopped you in the past?
- Are you happy with your current decision?
- Look at the questions in the section above and listen to your heart

This process may have helped you appreciate how wonderful your Life Canvas really is. It may have made you realise that there are still areas which have been neglected for too long, and which need attention. It may even help you listen to that voice inside which has been asking for change, and which you completely ignored. Don't forget that no one can avoid stress and pain at some point in their lives. There are benefits in stress, it can help you find your purpose in life, create future hope and the confidence to cope in future stressful situations.

In *The Art of Midlife Stress Busting* we can make the change only if our reason for doing so is PURE...

Positively Stated

Understood

Relevant

Ethical

When writing in your copy of *The Art of Stress Busting Companion* use positive language, and phrase it as if it has already happened. Make sure the reasoning is clearly defined and would be understood by those you love. Make sure your decision is relevant when weighed against all other matters. And most important of all, make sure that it is morally and ethically sound.

Next, take a piece of paper, and draw a vertical line down the middle. Add two headings: 'Pros' on the left side and 'Cons' on the right. Note all the reasons you can think of in the columns. Take your time, anything goes.

This exercise will help you with your decision.

If the list is longer in the 'Pro' column, check against your PURE answers to make sure you are changing your canvas for the right reasons.

Now is the time to put a plan of action together. Let your pen flow over your notebook until you have all the information you need. Use headings such as How, Who, What, Where and When to get you started.

Be aware of how much you have worked today. Give yourself a pat on the back and celebrate the day's journey in some way before you go to bed. You will then be ready for Step Six in *The Art of Midlife Stress Busting - Seven Steps to Declutter Your Mind Without Pills or Potions*.

Do ask for help if doing this work is too hard or painful for you.

Step Five Recap – Redecorating and Starting Anew

- Answer the questions above, so if you want to start your Life Canvas anew, you can do so PUREly
    - Seek help if you need it
    - Celebrate

Today we looked at starting a new canvas, the challenges you may face, and how to deal with them. Tomorrow we will look at how to become a Life Canvas Grand Master.

Step Six - Becoming A Grand Master

"Every artist was first an amateur." Ralph Waldo Emerson

Yesterday we looked at starting a new Life Canvas from scratch, and today we will look at how to become a Grand Master artist.

It's nearly the end of the week we set ourselves, so I have a question for you:

How do you walk 1,000 miles?

Step by step of course. How are you doing with your *Stress Busting* steps? Have you been taking everything one day at a time? Dedicating a little time each day to *The Art of Midlife Stress Busting* means that over a week you will have made great progress.

An artistic time-saving technique is to look at what other artists have done before you. Find someone who has 'been there and got the T-shirt'. Doing what they did can speed up a learning process. Yet there is an issue if you only copy someone else's life. They are not you and you are not them.

Following someone else's amazing life canvas *only* works to some extent, as we all paint completely different Life Canvases. At some point, you have to step away from the teachings of others and 'Do Your Own Thing'.

Imagine what the world would be like if we all attempted to be Picasso? What if we all copied Rembrandt? What a boring world that would be. We are all individuals. The aim is for each of us to be confident and passionate about what we do, and what we offer to others.

Who are you trying to be, apart from yourself?

You can only be yourself. Make sure you paint to the best of *your* ability every day, with passion and love. You only have one chance: the chance is NOW, TODAY. GO ON! Give it a whirl, and live today as if it's your last.

Becoming A Grand Master

The art of becoming a *Midlife Stress Busting* Grand Master is to find something which you are passionate about, and then learn and practise as much as you can. Be patient while you gain your artistic expertise for that particular topic.

Think of the names of famous masters that spring to your mind. To be a Grand Master takes many thousands of hours and true, unwavering dedication. Not only do you need to KNOW something, you need to BECOME it. The great thing about starting is that you are on your way to becoming a true Grand Master.

Continued perseverance is the key. A Grand Master understands that in order to make their special mark on the world, they must practice every day. Making sure their work of art is the best it can be requires the daily habit of attention.

Grand Masters of life must learn their art, first by taking note of the Grand Masters who have gone before them, and then learning from them. Then they must have the confidence to step out on their own and grow some more.

Each unique brushstroke will be a learning process, making the whole Life Canvas sparkle with light, depth, contrast, colour and texture.

Midlife Stress Busting Grand Masters are not afraid to make mistakes; they know this is where the real learning takes place. They are happy to constantly declutter so that they can work with the stress in their life. Grand Masters are not afraid to experiment, since they know this is where they can express their individuality. Grand Masters are able to decide for themselves and reach their own conclusions, without worrying about what others may think.

They pay attention to their thoughts, emotions and sensations and are happy to embrace stress in order to grow. They know that they cannot control everything in their lives, yet they can control the way in which they respond. Stress will challenge a Grand Master to find further meaning in their life.

A Grand Master is always available to help others, and to pass on knowledge. They are happy to learn a new point of view and apply it to their lives, and they embrace the opportunity to share it with others. More importantly, they are never afraid to ask for help in order to succeed. They understand how empathy works. Their desire to help others not only helps others to grow, it helps them to find meaning in their lives.

Grand Masters also understand the importance of spending time with their canvas on a daily basis. A quiet time contemplating what they see may be more important than actually attending to the paint. Contemplation enables a Grand Master to tap into their subconscious mind, and in so doing, find the answers they seek. Here is Cindy's contemplation:

"I never really understood the concept of being at peace; to just sit and contemplate and meditate, until I reached my late 40s. I suppose when I was young, free and single I didn't have the time or desire to sit and just be.

"When you marry and have kids, time never seems to be your own, and then all of a sudden you find yourself with an empty nest and you have more than enough time to spend with your mind!

"I am amazed at how my artwork has changed and grown since I hit my
mid-50s. Now, I seem to have an artwork that is multi-dimensional, not just flat. I know this, because people have commented, and what is more surprising, they have approached me and asked me how I do it!

"In a strange way, I am really looking forward to my body slowing down so I can spend more time working on my mind's artwork, de-stressing and getting rid of all my mind's clutter. I have a lot more work to do before I humbly accept the title of Midlife Stress Busting Grand Master; *but at least I'm on my way."*

Tasks For Today

Find a quiet place to sit. Make sure you have 20 minutes in which to do this exercise without being disturbed.

Begin by reading through the questions below, then close your eyes, and quietly contemplate your Life's Work of Art. Don't just look at it, but feel it, smell it, listen to it, touch it and even taste it. Think of it in terms of the seasons changing. See how your Life's Canvas has evolved into who you are today.

You are here today looking at what you have created. It's time to take stock of all those achievements, big or small. Look at how far you have come to be where you are today. You are well on your way to becoming a Life Canvas *Midlife Stress Busting* Grand Master.

Take a deep breath and look at your canvas in detail...

- What do you now need to do so you can move forward?
- Which places need care and attention?
- Which areas of the canvas need to be repainted or redefined?

Think about all the people who are included in your canvas, and all those who you know will include you in their Life Canvas...

- What would you like to do in order to help them become Grand Masters in their own right?

Think of all those Grand Masters who have gone before you...

- Who do you admire most?
- What can you learn from them?
- What teachings can you apply to your own life?

Think about your uniqueness...

- What do you offer the world that no one else can?
- What can others learn from you?

So how did this tasks go for you? Did you find it easy to sit still and contemplate? If you have never practised before you may find this difficult and frustrating.

Be aware of how much you have worked today. Give yourself a pat on the back and celebrate the day's journey in some way before you go to bed.

Step Six Recap – Becoming A Grand Master

- Find a place to contemplate quietly
- Answer the questions above
- Celebrate

Today we have learned from the Grand Masters, and know how to become one ourselves. Tomorrow is the final day, where we will look at beginning the whole cycle again. I hope you're excited.

Step Seven - Preparing For The Future

"The 'earth' without 'art' is just 'eh'." Unknown

Yesterday we looked at becoming a Life Canvas Grand Master, today we look at continuing the process.

Did you ever read the book *The Neverending Story* as a child? *The Art of Midlife Stress Busting* is just like that. The Good News is that it's a never-ending story, and the bad news is that it's never-ending. (See Resources).

A *Midlife Stress Busting* life is all about reflecting, making adjustments and beginning again. It's all about making sure you come from the right place in all that you create, so that you not only help yourself, you can also help those who you care about.

You must reflect, create and adjust all the time. Above all else, YOU MUST ENJOY the process. There is a fine line between anxiety and excitement. Always choose to be excited.

Stress is part of who you are. You cannot avoid it, yet you can control your mindset and the way you respond to it. Avoiding stress creates more stress, overwhelm, feelings of inadequacy, meaninglessness and isolation from others.

By embracing stress and continually working on your thoughts, your Life Canvas will always be at its best.

Full Circle

Step Seven is easy. Today is Total Reflection Day.

Today is all about reflecting on the previous six steps and, as a *Midlife Stress Busting* Grand Master, preparing to begin the cycle once again. Today is only easy if you actually put it into practice.

If you don't work on today's task, your efforts on the six previous days will be wasted.

Have a look at your notes in the *Companion* for this week, and underline anything that stands out for you. Are there any surprises? Has something totally unexpected happened? Are your newly-honed artistic skills already beginning to pay off?

Note: At this point you may want to treat yourself to another notebook, something that you can take with you everywhere, and use all year round when the urge is great. Make sure you choose a notebook you love and will want to use constantly. You need to make it your best friend, because you will be spending a lot of time together.

Now is the time to think about planning a celebration, and making plans and adjustments for the coming week.

I'm sure there's a reason why most religions have a day of rest. Those who stop and appreciate what they have achieved on their Life Canvas seem more capable of applying paint the following week, with even more aplomb.

As you learn to appreciate how far you've come in just one week, including the little achievements, just think how your Life Canvas will look in a month...two months...a year!

The more you celebrate, the easier it is to paint. By seeing the positive on your Life Canvas, you can achieve even more.

Tasks For Today

First Task

As you have worked through the tasks during the past seven days, you may have noticed that things in your life have moved for you. You may now be aware of some of those sticking points. You may have some more work to do.

The problem is that it's so easy to revert to old ways, so easy to stop writing things down, and stop making an effort. It's so easy to forget just how far you have travelled, so easy to throw away the paints and store your Life Canvas behind the TV.

So what's the secret to keep moving forwards?

Stress Busting Artists know the importance of celebrating even the tiniest step forward. Your task today is to plan - and take part in - a celebration.

- Where will you go?
- Who will come with you?
- What will you be celebrating?

It doesn't need to take up a lot of time, nor cost a fortune, but you must write down all that you intend to do, AND how you feel after celebrating.

Each week you will be able to see the change and feel the results. You will be able to compare your achievements with how things were the previous week, and you can celebrate this too.

You must celebrate ALL wins. No matter how small. Even the tiniest step forward. Celebrating all wins will help expand your comfort zones, and create growth like nothing else can.

Celebrate with someone else: your Stress Buster, best friend, partner or a family member (the cat or dog don't count). You must plan your celebration so that it can't be forgotten.

Write down all that you feel before and after your celebration, and visit those notes whenever you feel low, or when things are not going right for you.

Second Task

If you have found this useful, and know of someone else who would benefit from reading it, please let them know about this book. Helping others is a sure way of feeling positive about yourself. By passing on your good energy, you not only change your own life, you will change the lives of others.

Find someone new each week to gift this book to. Think about creating a local *Art of Midlife Stress Busting* coffee group where you can help each other do the work described in this book, and keep on track, accountable and celebrating together.

On this final day, you have learned about the importance of continued reflection and celebration, as well as passing on the message to others.

Thank you for persevering to the end.
I have two questions for you...

Have you only read this?
Or have you really implemented it?

If you have implemented it, you have achieved *The Art of Midlife Stress Busting* and taken the *Seven Steps to Declutter Your Mind Without Pills or Potions*, and you're aware how important it is to keep working on it regularly.

Welcome to your New Life, *FREE of unnecessary STRESS*!

Step Seven Recap – Preparing For The Future

- Review again and again
- Celebrate

Conclusion

Once again, congratulations, you have completed *The Art of Midlife Stress Busting - Seven Steps to Declutter Your Mind Without Pills or Potions*

Every week a *Stress Busting Artist* must use their skills in...

1. Awareness
2. Having the right equipment
3. Learning to Ready, Fire, Aim
4. Avoiding the two Ps
5. Redecorating and starting anew
6. Becoming a Grand Master
7. Repeatedly being prepared to come Full Circle

If you have found this work emotionally unsettling, or want to go deeper, please don't hesitate to contact me via kay@kay-newton.com

If you only read the book and truly want to make changes in your life, yet feel you need help, then check out the *Stress Bust Now* sessions at
https://www.kay-newton.com/stress-bust-now/

I am very keen to hear your stories. You may just be the inspiration that another person needs to paint their Life Canvas differently.

My favourite quote from a life Grand Master:

"Do, or do not. There is no try." Star Wars Jedi master, Yoda.

It has been a pleasure to spend time with you this week, and I hope to see more of you in the future. Sending love from my heart to yours.
Kx

Now see how the **resources** below may help you.

Resources

Find your values: https://www.kay-newton.com/values/

Recommended Reading
The Neverending Story:
http://www.amazon.com/The-Neverending-Story-Michael-Ende/dp/0140386335

To Find Kay

Website: https://www.kay-newton.com/
Facebook Page:
https://www.facebook.com/TheMidlifeStressBuster/
Facebook Group:
https://www.facebook.com/groups/MidlifeStressBusting

Other Books by Kay

How to Clean Your Home Organically – De-Stress Your Surroundings

https://www.amazon.com/Clean-Your-Home-Organically-stress-ebook/dp/B071VH9YP3

Tips And Tricks For Stress-Free Downsizing - A Step by Step Guide to Moving On

https://www.amazon.com/Tips-Tricks-Stress-Free-Downsizing-Moving-ebook/dp/B0722THJ3Z

To buy titles in the *Quick Fix Series* by Pat Duckworth and Kay Newton:

Quick Fix For Empty Nest Syndrome -
http://amzn.to/2pNRl8x

Quick For Parents Living With Boomerang Kids -
http://amzn.to/2pgxuM2

Quick fix For Giving Glorious Gifts -
http://amzn.to/2pd570A

Quick Fix For Your Meaningful Midlife Relationship -
http://amzn.to/2pNqVSc

Quick Fix For Decluttering -
http://amzn.to/2qzD8Nl

Quick Fix For Better Sleep -
http://amzn.to/2qHCA5a

Printed in Great Britain
by Amazon